DISCOVER LANDSCAPES

THE LAKE DISTRICT
South Lakes

Grasmere with the peaks of Helm Crag, Seat Sandal, Great Rigg and Rydal Fell reflected in the still waters of the lake

ROBERT GRANGE

MYRIAD

LONDON

LOUGHRIGG TERRACE

Grasmere is the most popular tourist village in the south lakes, thanks to its Wordsworth connections. On the south side of the lake, a picturesque path leads to Loughrigg Terrace which gives unsurpassed views of the surrounding countryside.

Halfway up Loughrigg Fell at the south end of Grasmere is an ancient path called the Terrace. It's a great place to sit and admire the view, especially in late spring with the hawthorn trees plastered with blossom. If the weather is kind, visitors will be able to enjoy the warmth of the sun and the gentle background music of birds and sheep on the fell. Looking north you can see the only gap in the Lakeland mountain range, Dunmail Raise, which divides the Langdale range of mountains on the left from the Helvellyn range on the right. The view here is made up of Seat Sandal, Great Rigg and Heron Pike.

RYDAL

Rydal Water is the "sister" of Grasmere – the two sit side-by-side, separated only by a narrow strip of land. Rydal Water has its own unique attractions: surrounded by marshy reed beds, and with a number of wooded islands, parts of the lake always remain hidden, giving it a mysterious atmosphere – especially when there is mist in the air.

Late summer mornings often have a cold bite to them and it is this which gives rise to the morning mist that lingers in the bottom of the valley. The silhouette of the tops of the trees can be made out across the lake below the sun-tinged outline of Loughrigg Fell.

Watching the mist rise off the water and seeing the power of the sun burn it away is a wonderful experience. Just before these photographs were taken, the mist was so thick you could not see for more than a few metres. But now as it lifts, it gives a black and white vision tinged with the red of the morning light. Heron Island is the largest of the islands of Rydal Water. These elegant birds are a common sight in the placid waters at the edge of the lake.

LOUGHRIGG AND THE LANGDALES

The Langdales – Great Langdale and Little Langdale – lie in picturesque valleys to the west of Grasmere. The area's distinctive rock-topped hills – the Langdale Pikes – are a great attraction for walkers. Loughrigg Tarn, a small stretch of water of almost unbelievable natural beauty, also lies in this area.

Loughrigg Tarn is one of those "chocolate box" settings. While lily pads brush the foreshore a flock of white ducks swim to a bank covered in ancient oak trees that turn red and orange in the autumn. Sheep graze in the meadows in the shadow of the stunning Langdale Pikes behind. As you walk back to the road you can glimpse a view of one of the old farmsteads that nestles in at the bottom of Loughrigg Fell.

RIVER BRATHAY

The river Brathay (the "broad river") rises in the Langdale valleys, flows eastwards past the village of Elterwater and finally empties into Windermere.

The slow moving river Brathay has a feel like no other waterway in the whole of the Lake District National Park. Here a wide-open pool edged by reeds and lily pads remains motionless in the morning light. The glacial moraines give high vantage points for the copses of trees that are surrounded by a network of meadows. This beautiful landscape, which has evolved over millions of years, certainly has a timeless quality about it.

Langdale has been a centre of human activity for many thousands of years. Not far from the location of this photograph ancient rock carvings are still clearly visible today. In the Stone Age rock of the highest quality was quarried from sites in the Langdales to make axe heads. These Stone Age artefacts have since been found all over Britain. It's thought they were the very best that could be traded at the time. Today Great Langdale is a wonderful centre for walkers, as it gives easy access to many of the fells. The most popular of them must be the gloriously named Harrison Stickle and Pike of Stickle, in the Langdale Pikes, pictured here.

PAVEY ARC

The Langdale Pikes with their rocky, dome-shaped tops are a favourite with visitors to the south lakes. Peaks with such distinctive names as Stickle Ghyll, Harrison Stickle, Loft Crag and Pike of Stickle appear in most walking guides. These mountains are well-known for their waterfalls – none more dramatic than Dungeon Gill.

High above the Langdale valley, nestled in between the peaks, is Stickle Tarn. On its north side is a famous climbing crag called Pavey Arc. This impressive piece of rock rises dramatically from the shoreline, making it a superb venue for anyone wanting to spend a day on the rock. For those whose nerves aren't quite made of steel there is an incredible scramble right across the front face of this crag. The path can just be seen starting on the bottom right and working its way through to the top left following the ledge known as Jacks Rake.

DUNGEON GILL

On the side of the Langdale Pikes is a well-known, if not frequently visited, waterfall called Dungeon Gill. Its name is synonymous with the hotel and bar at its foot, as this is the gateway to the Langdales for most walkers. The Gill tumbles its way down the hillside in a series of waterfalls and pools, with its most spectacular moment coming as it plunges about 70ft (21m) into a ravine. The overhanging cliffs on each side highlight the drama of this place. Just out of the top of this photograph a large boulder approximately 20ft (6m) across has become jammed at the top of the gorge some 100ft (30.5m) above the stream, giving a "tunnel-like" feel to this desolate spot.

LANGDALE PIKES

Many people have their first view of the Langdale Pikes as they approach Ambleside on the A591 and look across Windermere to see the distinctive shapes of the Pikes on the horizon. The view looking the other way – particularly from the top of one of the higher peaks – is even more dramatic. On a clear day, a walker on the Pikes can see the Pennines to the east while Windermere appears reduced to the size of a small stream.

From high up on Esk Hause, you can look back at the Langdale Pikes from above with the true dome shape of Pike of Stickle standing out in the afternoon light. In the distance you can see the Pennines capped in snow and Windermere, the largest lake in the Lake District, weaving out at the foot of the mountains.

The photograph (right) looks down into Langdale. The dark mound of the Pike of Stickle dominates the background and the summit of Harrison Stickle can be seen on the left.

LANGDALE PIKES

Looking down from the rock-domed heights of the Pikes into the Langdale Valley with the dramatic ridge of Harrison Stickle on the left.

THE TOP OF THE LAKES

The Lake District National Park is rightly famous for its lakes in their green tranquil surroundings, but as you rise to the higher peaks the landscape changes. Here on the top of Ill Crag next to Scafell Pike the landscape is covered in large red boulders. This photograph, in which the rose red rock contrasts with the smooth blue sky, was captured on the path which weaves its way through this formidable terrain.

SCAFELL PIKE

Scafell Pike attracts thousands of climbers every year. But it's a stiff eight-hour climb from ground level and not for the faint-hearted.

The most famous mountain in the Lake District is also the highest – Scafell Pike. Despite its stature (3,163ft/964m) it has few photogenic profiles. Seen here from Great Gable you can just make out the famous corridor route working its way through the many gullies and gouges on the north face. In the photograph below, taken from the shores of Wast Water, you can see the western face with Lingmell on the left, Scafell Pike in the middle at the top of Pike Crags and then Scafell on the right-hand side. The mountain takes on an orange tint with the bracken and grass having died off over winter and the first shoots of spring not quite breaking through.

WAST WATER

Wast Water is set in beautiful rugged countryside to the west of Scafell Pike. Its remote location often deters visitors but it is easily reached using small roads running eastwards up Wasdale off the A595. Wast Water is the deepest lake in England – at some points the lake bed is below sea level.

Just to the north-west of Ravenglass is Wasdale, a quiet valley that runs from the sea up to the foot of Great Gable and Scafell Pike. Unspoilt by the passage of time the view down this valley has hardly changed in centuries. The field system here, with its strange pattern of irregular shapes, is quite remarkable. In order to work the land the stones had to be removed, and these were piled up and then eventually made into walls to pen in the animals. The farmers would not want to move the stones further than they had to, so they would join the piles together, eventually using most of them up. You can still see some heaps which appear as wider sections or bulges in the walls in this view from the top of Great Gable at the head of the valley.

THE ESK ESTUARY

On the western fringes of Cumbria where the Lake District touches the sea is Ravenglass, a sleepy little village on the Esk estuary where fishing boats lie in the evening light. A port for many thousands of years Ravenglass was favoured by the Romans and, more recently, by the mines in the Esk valley which transported their goods to the coast by rail. Known affectionately as the la'al ratty, the railway is a narrow-gauge line that winds its way up from the sea to the village of Boot in the mountains.

Today, Ravenglass is a haven for leisure boats and the sandbanks along the rivers Mite and Irt provide a good mooring for many yachts and pleasure craft. In the evening the textures in the sand catch the light like ripples on water. The pattern underfoot reveals many tiny details of marine life which are so often overlooked.

DUDDON VALLEY

In the far south-west of the national park is the Duddon Valley which Wordsworth considered his favourite place in the Lakes. It runs north from the small town of Broughton in Furness on the Cumbrian coast through Ulpha and Seathwaite to the Hardknott Pass in the north. The Old Man of Coniston dominates the views from the valley towards the east.

The Duddon valley is one of the most beautiful in the southern lakes. At its top is the valley between Hardknott and Wrynose Pass. This is where the three historic counties of Westmorland, Cumberland and Lancashire, which make up modern Cumbria, meet. The valley then works its way south-west towards the sea. One of the valley's hidden treasures is a packhorse bridge which spans a deep pool with blue-green water – a favourite with bathers on a sunny summer's day. Next to the bridge is the picnic spot at Hinning House Close, the starting point for some beautiful forest walks.

KELLY HALL TARN

Kelly Hall Tarn is only a short distance from the road running up the west side of Coniston Water in an area known as Torver Back Common. A good approach for walkers is from Torver, starting on the Walna Scar road, a bridleway. A right fork eventually passes Goats Water with its impressive backdrop of climbing crags.

Above the village of Torver near Coniston a small pond was dammed some years ago. This has left a little tarn with wonderful views of the Old Man of Coniston. The common land of the village stretches as far as Coniston Water giving beautiful views across the lake to Grizedale Forest and the low rolling hills towards Hawkshead.

TORVER

This pretty view, with pinstripe fields beneath a sky of cottonwool clouds, was captured south of Torver on the road to Broughton in Furness. It shows the beauty of the low-lying hills – so different from the Old Man of Coniston, just a few miles away.

CONISTON

The town of Coniston is situated close to the northern end of Coniston Water. Behind the town, the Old Man of Coniston provides a dramatic backdrop to an area rich in literary associations and the history of water speed record attempts.

The Old Man of Coniston with its rugged, rock-strewn slopes, its fluted ridge carved out by the ice many years ago and battle scars from centuries of mining, dominates the surrounding landscape. At its foot is the village of Coniston and Coniston Water. This was the setting for Arthur Ransome's much-loved children's book *Swallows and Amazons*, which was subsequently filmed here, and also for the attempt on the world water speed record by Donald Campbell. It now plays host to the steam gondola and pleasure craft as can be seen here from the shore by Brantwood, the home of the 19th-century critic, writer and social reformer John Ruskin.

HAWKSHEAD

Hawkshead lies midway between the northern ends of Coniston and Windermere. It's a charming village which retains all the historic character so beloved of its two most famous inhabitants – William Wordsworth, who went to school here and Beatrix Potter whose famous home, Hill Top, is close by.

The charming village of Hawkshead is situated between Windermere and Coniston, just at the head of Esthwaite Water. The village has changed very little since the 17th century. It consists of a network of little streets and passageways opening out into various squares and courtyards. Since the days when the Romantic poet William Wordsworth and his brother attended school here a few more coffee shops and outdoor shops have appeared, but the charm of the village still remains. St Michael's Church stands above the village and has views over the village and valley to the southern end of the Helvellyn hills and Kirkstone Pass.

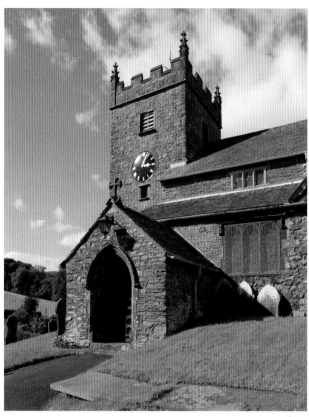

WINDERMERE

Windermere is England's longest lake stretching
10.5 miles (17km) from Ambleside in the north to
Staveley at its southern end. The town of Windermere,
the starting point for most visitors to the South Lakes,
is sited on its eastern shore.

Halfway down Windermere is a series of small islands that make a haven for countless boats on their moorings. A line of mountains rises above the lake – the oddly named Yoke is on the right, the more pronounced Bell is in the centre and, finally, High Street is on the left.

HEALD WOOD

In every corner of the Lake District there is a glade or pasture which is resplendent with bluebells in early spring. Heald Wood on the shores of Windermere is a magnificent bluebell wood. Here the species native to England can be found bathing in the half light of the forest floor next to the moss-clad root of an oak tree.

First published in 2010 by
Myriad Books Limited
35 Bishopsthorpe Road
London SE26 4PA

Photographs copyright © Robert Grange
Text copyright © Robert Grange

Robert Grange has asserted his right under the Copyright, Designs and Patents Act 1998 to be identified as the author of this work.

ISBN 1 84746 346 0   EAN 978 1 84746 346 3

Designed by Jerry Goldie
Printed in China
www.myriadbooks.com